Introduction and Cover Art Copyright 2008 – All rights reserved.

Although each page was copied from the original edition, this reprint is in no way endorsed by or associated with the Delmonico's. We hope for their continued success.

Since this was copied from a very very old original edition, the pages here may look a little funny at times. Rest assured we did our best to format the original book into modern form as best allowed by the current processes available.

This book, as always, is dedicated to my wife, friend, lover, and partner. And yes, they are all the same woman.

INTRODUCTION

Welcome to "Cheerio! A Book of Punches and Cocktails How to Mix Them 1928 Reprint".

This books was written by Charles, formerly of Delmonico's, who worked at the famous eatery at the heights of its fame. First publisheed right in the middle of prohibition, the author protryed the times of artful drinks as "gasping on its death-bed."

Perhaps written as a protest, perhaps written as a historical record, this book none the less captures a fantastic slice of history where drinks could be had if you knew the right "someone."

Forget about bar bibles or encyclopedias, what about drinks that people really used? As so few bar books were written and even fewer survived at all from the past 100 years, it a great pleasure to be able to bring these drinks that were used by the famous man Charles in the famous resteraunt Delmonico's to our modern attention and use.

Let's all raise our glass to Charles!

-Ross Bolton
May 8th, 2008

"CHEERIO!"

A BOOK OF PUNCHES AND COCKTAILS. HOW TO MIX THEM, AND OTHER RARE, EXQUISITE AND DELICATE DRINKS. INCLUDING A CHAPTER OF CELEBRITIES, THEIR FAVORITE DRINKS.

By CHARLES
Formerly of Delmonicos

ELF PUBLISHING COMPANY
1674 Broadway, N. Y. C.
1928

Copyright 1928
by
ELF PUBLISHING CO.
New York City

THE EIGHT IMMORTAL DRINKERS
By Tou-Fou (715-774)

Ho-Tchi-Tchang, always on horseback, looked like a man rowing a boat. One evening, when he was drunker than usual, he fell from his horse into a deep pit, and it is my belief that he is sleeping there yet.

Yu-Yang always empties three bottles before going to work. If he meets a grain cart he gives up all thought of business, follows along after it, and chats with the coolie about the fermentation of rice.

The minister, Li-Ti-Chy, could swallow a hundred rivers. He cheerfully spends ten million tsein, and declares that he would willingly cut off the heads of all merchants who sell dubious wine.

When Tsoung-Tchi savors a bottle only the whites of his eyes can be seen. Suddenly, there is a great noise! And there on the ground, like an uprooted tree, lies Tsoung-Tchi.

The solemn Sou-Tsin never drinks before the statue of Buddha. But once outside the Monastery, if he ever begins to drink, he must be carried back there on the shoulders of some charitable passerby.

Under the influence of a single measure of wine Li-Tai-Po is capable of writing three hundred verses. One day he was sleeping in the tavern of Tchang-nan when he received an order from the Emperor to come to the palace. "Say to the Emperor," answered he, "that I am talking with the gods."

When Tchang-Hio had emptied three cups he could handle the brushes with an inconceivable skill. At that moment, if all the kings of the earth were to enter his room, he would not budge.

Five big measures of wine carried the spirit of Tsaio-Soui to its greatest heights, and then the eloquence of our friend threw his guests into bewilderment.

Although I sometimes pledge them a draught I do not at all belong among these illustrious men, I who am more often made drunk by a ray from the moon.

—Translated from the Chinese by Franz Toussaint.

CONTENTS

Chapter		Page
	Introductory Note	7
I.	Morning Cocktails, Known as "Pickups" or "Bracers"	9
II.	Before and After Dinner Drinks	12
III.	Midnight and Before-Bed Drinks	15
IV.	"Tapering Off" Cocktails	18
V.	Ladies Cocktails and Other Delicacies	21
VI.	Temperance Drinks	24
VII.	Rare and Fancy Drinks	27
VIII.	Fancy Wine Drinks	31
IX.	Punches and Party Drinks	34
X.	Hot Drinks for the Fevered, Chilled and Cold	38
XI.	Celebrities Favorite Drinks	41
XII.	Miscellaneous Drinks for Anywhere and Anytime	44
	Index	48

INTRODUCTORY NOTE

This book has been written as much for the ordinary gentleman of good taste, as for the connoiseur or the epicure or the gourmet of drink. It is written, not with the crude and rough hand of any careless bartender, but with the fastidious and delicate hand of one who has served drinks to Princes, Magnates and Senators of many wealthy nations.

When that old vintner, Noah, first squeezed the precious grape into the cup, and throwing back his head, felt the vigorous wine-drops trickling deliciously down his parched throat, a new art was born, fostered and loved by Kings and Rajahs, flourishing in the courts of Emperors and Khans. And even today, if you observe in any street of any city, a man, more imaginative, more bold, more firm than his fellow men, you may depend upon it, he is descended direct from old Noah.

Today, that Art of creating exquisite drinks to match exquisite moods is gasping on its death-bed, and the dull ogre, Puritanism, supplanting the Skeleton, sits gloating by the bed-side, waiting eagerly to hear the last death-rattle.

If this volume succeeds in preserving, even a little while longer, that ancient and much beloved Art, the writer will be happy.

CHAPTER I.

MORNING DRINKS KNOWN AS "PICKUPS" OR "BRACERS"

When You Stagger Out of Bed, Groggy, Grouchy and Cross-Tempered

CHARLESTON BRACER

Place in shaker, one part brandy, one part Port wine, one raw egg, one-half teaspoonful of powdered sugar or plain syrup. Add sufficient cracked ice, shake thoroughly in order to break egg and strain into serving glass.

BRANDY SOUR

Mix in a small bar glass a large teaspoonful of powdered sugar dissolved in a little seltzer water, the juice of half a lemon, and a dash of Curacoa. Pour in a wine-glass of brandy. Fill the glass with shaved ice. Shake and strain into a claret glass. Ornament with orange and berries in season.

GIN SOUR

Mix in a small bar glass a large teaspoonful of powdered white sugar dissolved in a little seltzer water, the juice of half a lemon, and a dash of bitters. Pour in a wine-glass of gin. Fill the glass with shaved ice.

Shake and strain into a claret glass. Ornament with pineapple and berries in season.

Stinger

To two-thirds of brandy, add one-third of white Creme de Menthe. Ice, shake well, and serve in cocktail glass.

Dubonnet Cocktail

Mix in container two-thirds part Dubonnet, one-third dry gin, fill with ice, stir well, but do not shake, and strain into cocktail glass.

Jamaica Glow

In shaker place one part gin, one-half portion Claret, one-half portion orange juice, three or four dashes of Jamaica ginger. Fill with ice, shake thoroughly until very cold, strain in cocktail glass.

Pearl Cocktail

Two parts dry gin, one part French Vermouth, three dashes of onion juice, three dashes orange bitters. Shake well and strain into cocktail glass. Garnish with an olive.

Tom Collins

In a long tumbler, place one portion dry Gordon gin, juice of one-half lemon, one teaspoonful of powdered sugar, a few lumps of ice and seltzer water. Stir well.

North and South Cocktail

In shaker place one part Jamaica rum, and one part dry gin, juice of one orange or one-half lemon, and a dash of bitters. Ice, shake thoroughly and strain into glass.

Minute Man Highball

In a large tumbler mix one-half applejack, one-half Port wine and the juice of half an orange. Add ice and seltzer water. Ginger ale may be used if preferred.

Brandy Port Nog

Place in a shaker one part brandy, one part Port wine, one raw egg, one teaspoonful of powdered sugar. Fill the shaker with ice, shake thoroughly in order to break up the egg, then strain into a large cocktail glass. Grate a little nutmeg on top before serving.

Jamaica Bitters

Mix in a large glass a large teaspoonful of powdered sugar dissolved in a little seltzer water, three dashes of lemon juice and a wine-glass of Jamaica rum. Fill the glass with shaved ice, shake up and strain into a claret glass. Ornament with orange and berries in season.

CHAPTER II.

BEFORE AND AFTER DINNER DRINKS
For the Perfect Beginning and the Perfect Ending

ORANGE BLOSSOM SPECIAL

Dip a spoon in honey and dissolve the honey that adheres to the spoon in one part of gin. Add one part orange juice. Ice in shaker and strain into cocktail glass.

ORANGE BLOSSOM COCKTAIL

Add the juice of half an orange to one portion of gin; fill with ice, shake well and serve in cocktail glass.

MARTINI COCKTAIL

Place in shaker two parts dry gin, one part Italian Vermouth (French Vermouth if the drink is preferred dry), two dashes of orange bitters; fill with ice, shake and strain into a cocktail glass and garnish with a twist of lemon peel.

MINT SPRAY COCKTAIL

To one part of gin in a shaker add one part orange juice and a half teaspoonful of powdered sugar; add ice, and shake up thoroughly. Serve in cocktail glass, garnished with fresh mint.

BEFORE AND AFTER DINNER DRINKS

AMBER DREAM

Two-thirds dry gin, one-third French or Italian Vermouth, add a small portion of Chartreuse and a dash of orange bitters. Place in a shaker with ice, stir and serve.

HOLLAND OLD FASHIONED

Place a lump of sugar in a three ounce glass, reduce to syrup with a little hot water, a pony of Holland gin, two dashes of bitters, add a twist of lemon peel and a cube of ice. Stir slowly with a spoon and serve.

TOM GIN MARTINI

One-half part of Tom gin, one-half part Italian Vermouth, (French if you prefer dry) fill with ice, shake and serve with a green olive.

MINT JULEP

Dissolve one tablespoonful of powdered sugar in a portion of Bourbon in which a few sprigs of mint have been crushed. Add ice and seltzer water, and decorate with fresh mint.

HAVANA SPECIAL COCKTAIL

In shaker place three parts Bacardi rum and one part Grenadine, juice of one lime, shake well with ice, strain into cocktail glass and serve.

Alabama Mint Julep

Place a teaspoonful of granulated sugar in a small glass and pour in enough hot water to make a thick syrup. Pour this slowly into a shaker over cracked ice. Next place two ounces of Bourbon whiskey in shaker, along with three or four sprigs of mint which have been bruised between the thumb and forefinger. Shake well and serve in whiskey glass.

Apple Brandy Cocktail

Two-thirds apple brandy to one-third of Vermouth. Add a tablespoonful of syrup and a few dashes of orange bitters. Ice, shake well and serve in cocktail glass.

Brandy Smash

Dissolve spoonful of sugar in bottom of whiskey glass. Crush a few sprigs of mint in it. Add a portion of brandy and a piece of ice. Stir with spoon and serve with spoon in glass.

Country Cocktail

In shaker place a pony of Rye whiskey, two dashes orange bitters and two dashes Angostura bitters. Twist a piece of lemon peel and drop into container. Fill with crushed ice, mix well and strain into whiskey glass.

CHAPTER III.

MIDNIGHT AND BEFORE-BED DRINKS
For Insomnia, Bad Dreams, Disillusionment and Despair

GOLDEN FIZZ

In container place one portion of dry gin, the yolk of a raw egg and two teaspoonfuls of powdered sugar. Fill with ice, shake thoroughly to combine ingredients and serve with cold seltzer water. Drink while still effervescent.

HOT SPICED RUM

Fill a tumbler two-thirds full of hot water after placing spoon in glass and mix in a pony of Jamaica rum. Add one teaspoonful of sugar, juice of a quarter of a lemon, and whole cloves to suit taste. Serve with spoon.

EGG NOG

To one glass of fresh milk in a container add a raw egg, two teaspoonfuls of sugar, a pony of brandy, fill with ice and shake thoroughly to combine ingredients. Serve cold with a little grated nutmeg on top.

ALBERMARLE COCKTAIL

One pony Holland gin to one-half ounce Absinthe. Fill shaker with ice, shake and strain into cocktail glass.

CRIMSON COCKTAIL

Mix in a shaker one part dry gin with a dash of orange bitters. Ice, shake and pour into a glass. Then pour over this a half portion of Port wine. Allow it to settle without stirring before serving.

GIN AND ITALIAN

In a shaker pour two parts dry gin, one-third Italian Vermouth, juice of one-quarter of an orange and a sprig of mint. Fill with ice, shake well and strain into cocktail glass.

HOT IRISH

Fill a tumbler two-thirds full of boiling water, putting a spoon in glass first to prevent cracking. In this dissolve a spoonful of sugar and add a portion of Irish whiskey. Squirt in the juice of a quarter lemon, and ornament with a slice of lemon. Serve with a spoon.

EGG WHISKEY FIZZ

In a shaker place one portion whiskey, juice of half a lemon, a teaspoonful of powdered sugar, white of one raw egg, and a few dashes of Absinthe. Ice, shake thoroughly to combine ingredients and serve, half filling the glass. Fill up with seltzer water.

TOM AND JERRY

To one portion of brandy or rum, add one well-beaten raw egg and two teaspoonfuls of sugar. Stir thoroughly while pouring in hot milk, and serve with grated nutmeg or paprika on top.

Cholera Cocktail

In a bar glass pour half a teaspoonful of Jamaica ginger, one-third brandy, one-third Port wine and one-sixth each of Cherry and Blackberry brandy. Grate nutmeg on top and stir with spoon. Use no ice.

Egg Bacardi Rum Cocktail

In shaker place one dash Grenadine, one part Bacardi rum, one part lemon juice and white of one egg. Ice, shake until very cold and strain slowly.

Cold Brandy Flip

Mix together in a large glass a teaspoonful of powdered sugar, a wine-glass of brandy, a half wine-glass of water, a fresh raw egg and a few small lumps of ice. Shake up thoroughly, strain into a small bar glass and serve cold with a little grated nutmeg on top.

Sherry and Egg

Break one raw egg into a large glass, stir it up well and fill the glass with Sherry.

CHAPTER IV.

"TAPERING OFF" COCKTAILS

To Regain the Tight-Rope Walker's Balance, the Juggler's Hair Split Precision

Brandy and Soda

Into a large glass pour one wine-glass of brandy and add a few small lumps of ice. Fill up the glass with plain soda water. This is sometimes called a Stone Wall.

Whiskey Sour

Use a small bar glass. To a large teaspoonful of powdered sugar dissolved in a little seltzer water, add the juice of a small lemon. Pour in a wine-glass of Bourbon or Rye whiskey. Fill the glass full of shaved ice, shake up and strain into a claret glass. Ornament with berries before serving.

White Plush

Pour a small glass half full of Bourbon or Rye whiskey. Fill the glass with fresh milk. Drink without stirring.

Orange Gin Sparkle

One and a half ounces of gin, three dashes of orange

bitters, one dash Angostura bitters; twist piece of lemon peel and place in container, add ice and shake well. Before serving add a squirt of syphon seltzer.

Palm Beach Special

Two-thirds dry gin, one-sixth grapefruit juice, one-sixth either French or Italian Vermouth. Place in shaker, add ice. Shake well and serve in cocktail glass.

Gin Rickey

One portion Gordon gin in tumbler, juice of half a lime. Leave lime in glass with cracked ice and add soda water.

Gin and Italian with Sherry

Use shaker. One-half portion gin, one-half portion Italian Vermouth, exactly one tablespoonful Sherry, one dash of bitters. Fill with ice, mix, shake and strain.

Whiskey Fruit Cocktail

In shaker place one part Scotch or Rye, one part orange or grapefruit juice. Ice, shake well and serve. One dash of Angostura bitters if added will enhance the delicacy of the taste.

Planter's Punch

Use long glass. Squirt in the juice of a fresh lime,

two portions of sugar, a pony of water, four portions of old Jamaica rum. Fill glass with shaved ice, shake well, add dash of a red pepper if desired, and serve very cold with long straws.

Jamaica Rum Cocktail

A full pony of Jamaica rum, two dashes gum syrup, two dashes orange bitters, two dashes Angostura bitters, ice, shake and pour into cocktail glass.

Plymouth Cocktail

Two parts Plymouth gin, one-third Italian or French Vermouth, fill with ice. Shake well and serve with a twisted piece of lemon or orange peel.

CHAPTER V.

LADIES COCKTAILS AND OTHER DELICACIES
The Women Will No Doubt Speak for Themselves

ALEXANDER COCKTAIL

In a shaker place one-third gin, one-third Creme de Cocoa, and one-third rich cream. Fill with ice and shake well in order to get a thorough mixture. Strain and serve in cocktail glass.

CORONATION COCKTAIL

In shaker place one-third dry gin, one-third Cointreau Triple Sec and one-third white Creme de Menthe. Shake up thoroughly so as to mix cordials. Chop in ice, fine but not too fine. Strain into cocktail glass.

ORANGE CURACOA COCKTAIL

In container mix one part gin, one part orange gin, three dashes Curacoa, sweeten with half a teaspoonful of powdered sugar or honey, fill with ice and stir well before serving.

CORAL COCKTAIL

In shaker place two parts gin, one part French or Italian Vermouth and half a teaspoonful of Five Fruits syrup. Ice, shake well and serve in cordial glass.

Russet Cocktail

In a cocktail shaker place one part sweet cider, one part dry gin, and a teaspoonful of Grenadine or raspberry syrup. Add a few pieces of ice, shake well and strain into cocktail glass.

Port Wine Flip

Pour one portion of Port wine in container, one teaspoonful of powdered sugar, one raw egg well beaten, ice and shake thoroughly. Serve with grated nutmeg or cinnamon on top.

Egg Port Cocktail

One part Port wine, one raw egg, and two dashes of bitters. Fill with shaved ice, shake thoroughly to stir up egg in the container and strain into cocktail glass before serving.

Sherry Mint Cocktail

Place a pony of Sherry wine in a cocktail shaker, cut in two fine sprays of mint, add a dash of lemon or lime juice, shake well and strain into Delmonico glass after cold icing.

Duchess Cocktail

Place one-third each of French and Italian Vermouth and one-third Asbinthe in shaker. Fill with ice, shake well and serve in Delmonico glass.

Pousse Cafe

Pour carefully into a long thin cordial glass the following in rotation: raspberry syrup, orange Curacoa, green Creme de Menthe and brandy. Other combinations of cordials may be effected, always bearing in mind that the heaviest should be poured first and always end with brandy.

Queen of Ireland

Place two-thirds green Creme de Menthe in shaker, one-third Vermouth and one dash of orange bitters; fill with ice, shake well to get a smooth mixture and strain into cocktail glass.

Vermouth Cocktail

Place in container one portion of Italian Vermouth, one dash of bitters, fill with ice, shake and strain into cocktail glass.

Fancy Sour Cocktail

In shaker place one portion Vermouth, three dashes of Maraschino, four dashes of bitters and a dash of orange bitters. Squirt in juice of a quarter of a lemon. Fill with ice, shake and strain into cocktail glass.

CHAPTER VI.

TEMPERANCE DRINKS
Whenever the Stoic Spirit of Denial Seizes You

PURPLE NECTAR

Into a pitcher pour three pints of ginger ale. Add one-half pint of plain grape juice. Ice well and squeeze in half a lemon. Remove ice when sufficiently cold to serve.

AMBROSIA

In a pitcher of iced water, dip a small bag of tea until the water is slightly flavored. Add four spoonfuls of sugar. Cut up an orange into small pieces and allow to float in the drink. Then stir up with three spoonfuls of orange marmalade. Serve cold.

MILK FIZZ

Fill an ordinary water glass three-fourths full of ginger ale, add the rest milk. Stir with a spoonful of honey and drink cold.

NECTAR FOR DOG DAYS

Place a snow-ball of shaved ice in a goblet, squirt lemon juice over it and pour iced soda water over it till goblet is filled. This is a refreshing thirst quencher.

TEMPERANCE DRINKS

Saratoga Cooler

Mix in a large glass one bottle of ginger ale just off the ice, juice of half a lemon, and one teaspoonful of powdered sugar.

Soda Cocktail

In bottom of a large glass pour one teaspoonful of powdered sugar, three or four lumps of ice, and two dashes of Angostura bitters. Pour over these ingredients a cold bottle of soda water, stir and remove ice before serving.

Iced Sarsaparilla

Mix in a small pitcher two bottles of sarsaparilla, juice of half a lemon and add plenty of ice. Serve very cold.

Soda Nectar

One glass of soda water, add a squirt of lemon juice, ice and add two or three drops of vanilla extract.

Milk and Seltzer

Fill half a glass with cold milk, and the rest with iced seltzer. Drink while effervescent.

Cider Cocktail

In a Delmonico glass place one-half a teaspoonful of sugar, add two dashes of bitters, twist in a piece of lemon peel, add a few lumps of ice, fill with cider, and stir well before serving.

TEMPERANCE DRINKS

Phosphate Special

In a container pour three-fourths of non-alcoholic Vermouth, three dashes of phosphate, three dashes of orange bitters, fill with cracked ice, shake well and strain into cocktail glass.

Oggle Noggle

Beat a whole raw egg into a glass of boiling milk. Add a spoonful of sugar and a small lump of butter big as the end of your fingernail. Stir well and serve hot. This is a healthy and refreshing drink for growing children.

Lemonade

Squeeze two or three pieces of orange and half a lemon into a large glass or small bowl. Fill with water and add ice. Add two spoonfuls of sugar. Allow pieces of lemon and orange to float in bowl together with three or four Maraschino cherries.

Egg Lemonade

In a large glass mix juice of half a lemon, one teaspoonful of powdered sugar, one raw egg, and three or four small pieces of ice. Stir up thoroughly in a shaker, strain into a soda-water glass and fill up with seltzer water. Ornament with berries and serve cold.

CHAPTER VII.

RARE AND FANCY DRINKS

For Impish, Elfish, Mad, Capricious, Fairy Whims

Absinthe Frappe

Scrape ice fine as snow. Place in flat wine-glass and cover with a pony of Absinthe; serve with short straw and suck slowly as ice melts.

Peach and Honey

Over a tablespoonful of raw honey, pour a wine-glass of Peach brandy. Stir thoroughly and sip slowly.

Bishop

In a large glass pour one wine-glass of water in which a teaspoonful of powdered sugar has been dissolved. Add two thin slices of lemon, two dashes of Jamaica rum and a few small lumps of ice. Fill the glass with Claret or red Burgundy, shake well and remove ice before serving.

Brandy Fizz

Mix in a glass a teaspoonful of powdered sugar, three dashes of lemon juice, and a small lump of ice. Pour in a wine-glass full of brandy. Fill up the glass with seltzer water, stir thoroughly and serve while effervescent.

Brandy Smash

Press three or four sprigs of tender mint into the bottom of a glass in which some sugared water has been placed. Add a wine-glass full of brandy and fill the glass two-thirds full of shaved ice. Stir thoroughly and ornament with half a slice of orange, and a few fresh sprigs of mint. Serve with a straw.

English Bishop

Roast an orange which has been stuck well with cloves over a fire, and when sufficiently brown, cut it into quarters and pour over it a bottle of heated Port wine. Add a spoonful of honey and let the mixture simmer over the fire for twenty minutes. Then serve piping hot.

Silver Fizz

In a container place one portion of dry gin, the white of an egg, two teaspoonfuls of powdered sugar, three dashes of lemon juice. Fill with ice and shake thoroughly to combine the ingredients. Serve in a tumbler with seltzer water.

Ramos Fizz

Pour in a shaker, one portion of dry gin, juice of half a lemon, white of one egg, one teaspoonful of powdered sugar, a few dashes of orange bitters. Fill with ice and mix thoroughly to combine the ingredients. Serve in a tumbler with soda water.

Fancy Whiskey Cocktail

Place in shaker one pony Rye whiskey, add two dashes Maraschino, two dashes bitters, one dash orange bitters and fill with ice until very cold. Shake and strain into small whiskey glass.

Carlton Brandy Cocktail

In a shaker place a pony of brandy, add three dashes of Maraschino and two dashes of bitters. Fill with ice and shake. Pour into cocktail glass which has been prepared by moistening its rim with a slice of lemon dipped in powdered sugar.

Locomotive

In a mug thoroughly beat together the yolk of a raw egg, a tablespoonful of honey and three dashes of Curacoa. Heat a claret glass of red Burgandy in a thoroughly clean sauce-pan until it boils, and then pour it gradually upon the other ingredients, whisking and stirring the ingredients all the while in order to prevent curdling. Serve hot.

Sazarac Cocktail

To one portion of whiskey, add three or four **dashes**

of Absinthe, one tablespoonful of plain syrup, three dashes of bitters. Ice, shake well and serve in whiskey glass, garnished with a sprig of mint which has been bruised between the thumb and forefinger.

Cuban Bacardi

In container pour one wine-glass of Bacardi rum, add white of one egg, large tablespoonful of pineapple juice, same amount of orange juice. Fill shaker three-quarters full of cracked ice, shake rapidly a few times and serve.

Champagne Cup

Into a pitcher place a quart of Champagne, two ponies of brandy, two teaspoonfuls of powdered sugar, a wine-glass of Sherry, and a dash of Curacoa and Maraschino. Add pieces of pineapple, orange, and berries in season. Garnish with fresh mint and serve in champagne goblet.

Whiskey Smash

Mix together a teaspoonful of powdered sugar, dissolved in a little water, a wine-glass of whiskey, and put in three or four sprigs of young mint which have been bruised between the thumb and forefinger.

CHAPTER VIII.

FANCY WINE DRINKS

For the Pink-Jowled, Round-Paunched, Side-Whiskered Lover of Red, Gold, Purple and Plain White Wines

Rajah

Roast four bitter oranges until they are of a pale brown color. Lay them in a tureen and cover them with a half pound of granulated sugar, adding three glasses of Claret. Cover the tureen and let it stand until the next day. Then place the tureen in a pan of boiling water, press the oranges with a spoon, until the juice spurts, and run the juice through a sieve to strain it clear. Add to it two glassfuls of boiling Claret and serve warm in goblets. Port wine may be substituted for Claret, and lemons may be used instead of oranges, but this is not often done when Claret is used.

Mulled Muscatel

Into a pot of boiling water put a suitable quantity of cloves, cinnamon and grated nutmeg. When the flavor becomes pungent to the nostrils pour in an equal amount of Muscatel wine in which a few teaspoonfuls of sugar have been dissolved. Bring the whole to the boiling point, and serve piping hot with crisp dry toast. Mulled wine can be made with Port, Claret or Madeira.

FANCY WINE DRINKS

Claret Cup

Mix into a container one bottle of Claret wine, a half pint of iced water, a tablespoonful of powdered sugar, and one teaspoonful of powdered cinnamon, cloves and allspice, mixed. Squirt in the juice of a small lemon. Stir the ingredients well together, adding the thin rind of the lemon. This is a delicate summer beverage for evening parties.

Sherry Egg Nog

Pour into a large bar glass two wine-glasses of Sherry wine, a well-beaten egg and fill rest with rich creamy milk. Add a few lumps of ice. Stir thoroughly and strain into a large goblet. Grate a little nutmeg on top and remove ice before serving.

Rhine and Seltzer

Fill a glass half full of Rhine wine. Add ice and fill up with seltzer water. Serve very cold. This is an excellent thirst quencher.

Sherry Cobbler

Into a large glass put one tablespoonful of powdered white sugar, one-quarter of an orange cut up into pieces and two small pieces of pineapple. Fill the glass nearly full of shaved ice, then fill up with Sherry wine. Ornament the top with berries in season, and serve with straws.

Champagne Cobbler

Fill container one-third full of shaved ice, throw in a piece of orange or lemon peel, fill up with Champagne, ornament with berries in season and serve with straws.

Baclanova Nectar

In a large container peel and shred fine the rind of half a lemon, add a tablespoonful of powdered sugar and the juice of a whole lemon. Cut in a few thin slices of cucumber with the peel on. Add a bottle of Claret, a pint of Champagne and a bottle of seltzer water. Fill with ice, stir thoroughly and serve.

Sherrio Cocktail

To one part of Sherry wine add an equal amount of Vermouth, two dashes of orange bitters, place in a shaker with ice, and stir thoroughly and serve.

Champagne Cocktail

In a goblet place one lump of loaf sugar saturated with Angostura bitters, one cube of ice and one piece of twisted lemon peel. Fill the goblet with cold Champagne, stir with a spoon and serve.

Port Wine Sangaree

Into a glass of Port wine put in a half teaspoonful of powdered sugar, and add a few small lumps of ice. Shake up well, strain into a claret goblet and serve with a little grated nutmeg on top.

CHAPTER IX.

PUNCHES AND PARTY DRINKS

For Those Who See in the Bottom of a Punchbowl a Horoscope of Gaiety, Joy, Revelry, Carousing and Happy Madness

NECTAR PUNCH

Into a small punch bowl pour a quart of rum, one pint of milk boiling-hot, one quart of cold water, and a pound of granulated sugar. Cool gradually and add ice. Add a few slices of apple before serving.

PUNCH A LA ROMAINE

For a party of fifteen to twenty persons, dissolve two pounds of powdered sugar in the juice of ten lemons and two sweet oranges, adding the thin rind of one orange. Strain this through a sieve into a large punch bowl and add the white of ten eggs beaten to a froth. Place the bowl on ice for a while, then stir in briskly a quart of rum, and two bottles of Port wine. Do not serve too cold.

CLARET PUNCH

Fill a tumbler two-thirds full of shaved ice, add a teaspoonful of powdered sugar, a slice of lemon and a slice of orange, both cut into quarters; fill with Claret, shake well, and ornament with berries in season. Serve with a straw.

Sauterne Punch

Fill a small container two-thirds full of shaved ice. Add one teaspoonful of powdered sugar, one slice of lemon, one slice of orange, one piece of pineapple. Fill with Sauterne, ornament with berries in season and serve with a straw.

Champagne Punch

Mix together in a container, one quart of Champagne, three tablespoonfuls of sugar, one orange sliced, the juice of a lemon, two slices of pineapple cut into small pieces and a wine-glass measure of raspberry or strawberry syrup. Put in a few lumps of ice. Ornament with fruits in season and serve in champagne goblets after removing ice.

Orange Punch

Cut the peel of two oranges into a quart and a half of water and squeeze in the juice of four oranges; also drop in a small cupful of powdered sugar. Allow to boil half an hour and add a half pint of porter, three-quarters of a pint of rum and an equal amount of brandy. A liqueur glass of Curacoa and a dash of Maraschino will improve the drink immensely. Serve piping hot. Lemon Punch may be made with this formula by substituting lemons for oranges.

Brandy Punch

Into a punch bowl mix a teaspoonful of powdered sugar dissolved in a little water, a teaspoonful of raspberry syrup, a wine-glass of brandy, half a wine-glass of Jamaica rum, juice of half a lemon, two slices of orange and a piece of pineapple. Fill the bowl with shaved ice, stir thoroughly and dress the top with berries in season. Serve with a straw.

Hot Brandy and Rum Punch

This is an excellent punch for a party of fifteen coming in from cold and biting weather. Rub a pound of white loaf sugar over four lemons until it has absorbed all the yellow part of the skins, then put the sugar into a large punch bowl, stirring it together with the lemon juice. Pour three quarts of boiling water over this, adding a quart of Jamaica rum, a quart of brandy and a teaspoonful of grated nutmeg. Mix thoroughly and the punch will be ready to serve.

Milk Punch

In a large glass pour a teaspoonful of white sugar, a wine-glass full of brandy, one-half wine-glass of rum and a small lump of ice. Fill the glass with milk, shake well and grate a little nutmeg on top before serving.

Imperial Punch

Into a large pitcher pour a bottle of Claret, a bottle of soda water, four tablespoonfuls of powdered sugar, a quarter teaspoonful of grated nutmeg, and a liqueur glass of Maraschino. Put in a few large lumps of ice and three or four slices of cucumber rind. Mix well and serve.

St. Charles Punch

In a large glass pour one teaspoonful of sugar dissolved in a little water, one wine-glass of Port wine, one pony of brandy and the juice of a quarter of a lemon. Fill the glass with shaved ice, stir well, ornament with fruits in season and serve with a straw.

El Dorado Punch

Pour into a large glass a pony of brandy, a half pony of Jamaica rum, a half pony of Bourbon, and add a tablespoonful of sugar and a slice of lemon. Fill the glass with fine ice, stir well and ornament with berries and small pieces of orange. Serve with a straw.

Claret Cup A La Henry VIII

Peel off the rind of a lemon and mix both the juice and rind with powdered sugar. Pour over them a glass of Sherry and a bottle of Claret and sweeten to taste. Add a sprig of verbena and a bottle of soda water with a little grated nutmeg. Strain the mixture and serve with ice.

CHAPTER X.

HOT DRINKS FOR THE FEVERED, CHILLED AND COLD

For Wet Feet, Chattering Teeth, Cold Spines, Shivers, Goose-Flesh, Frozen Fingers and Chillbain

BLUE BLAZER

Use two glass mugs. In one dissolve a teaspoonful of powdered sugar with a wine-glass of boiling water. Pour in one wine-glass of Scotch whiskey. Ignite the liquid with fire, and while blazing mix the ingredients by pouring from one mug to the other, four or five times. If expertly done it will have the appearance of a continued stream of fire, but the novice should be careful not to scald himself. Serve piping hot in a small glass with a piece of twisted lemon peel.

HOT RUM

In a heated bar glass pour one wine-glass of Jamaica rum. Add a teaspoonful of powdered sugar and a small piece of butter, big as the end of your fingernail. Fill with boiling water, stirring as you pour. Grate a little nutmeg on top and serve.

PORT WINE NEGUS

Pour a large glass of Port wine into a pitcher. Rub

five or six lumps of sugar against the rind of a lemon until all the yellow part of the skin is absorbed by the sugar. Squeeze the lemon juice on the sugar, strain, and add the lemon juice and sugar to the Port wine. Add grated nutmeg, fill up with boiling water, cover the whole, and when cooled off it will be ready to serve.

Hot Whiskey Toddy

Dissolve a teaspoonful of sugar with boiling water in a large bar glass. Add one wine-glass of Bourbon or Rye whiskey, and fill up with boiling water.

Hot Gin Sling

Dissolve a small spoonful of powdered sugar in a little boiling water, add a wine-glass of gin, and fill up with boiling water. Grate a little nutmeg on top and serve.

Rock and Rye

Stir together in a small container one tablespoonful of rock-candy syrup and one wine-glass full of Rye whiskey. Heat over a flame and drink hot. This is excellent for a cold.

Hot Italian

Pare the rind of four lemons, and squeeze the juice upon the peel, steeping it overnight. Then add half a pound of loaf sugar, a large glass of Sherry wine and a large glass of boiling water. Stir well, add three large glasses of boiling milk, strain through a cloth and serve piping hot.

HOT SCOTCH PUNCH

Mix in a large glass, one wine-glass of Scotch whiskey, two wine-glasses of boiling water. Add two lumps of sugar and serve.

HOT IRISH WHISKEY PUNCH

Mix in large glass, one wine-glass of Irish whiskey, two wine-glasses of boiling water, two lumps of sugar. Put in a small piece of lemon rind or a thin slice of lemon. Before using the glass, rinse it in hot water.

HOT BRANDY TODDY

Dissolve a teaspoonful of powdered sugar in a little boiling water, add brandy and fill up with boiling water. Add a little grated nutmeg on top and serve.

HOT APPLEJACK

Fill a container two-thirds full of boiling water, and one-third full of applejack. Squirt in juice of one quarter of a lemon, add two spoonfuls of sugar, garnish with a slice of lemon and serve.

CHAPTER XI.

CELEBRITIES FAVORITE DRINKS

What Some of Our Best Known People Drink When They Are Abroad

BEN BERNIE, Orchestrian Extraordinary.
"In London I have found an excellent Chablis. In Berlin at times I have enjoyed something like a 'Sauterne Cobbler'. It is made by filling a container with Sauterne, adding shaved ice, and throwing in a few white cherries and small pieces of pineapple to give it color. Travel is not without its benefits."

WINNIE LIGHTNER, international star of musical shows.
"When I was playing in London I used to call for a drink that all my friends laughed at, but after a while they began to call it the 'Lightner Special.' Absinthe and Canada Dry ginger ale stirred up together in a glass. Can you imagine it?"

"BIG BILL" TILDEN, most famous of Tennis stars.
"I use only water."

CHARLES WINNINGER, musical comedy star.
"Have you heard of the "Pousse l'Amour?" Try it at the Cafe du Dome in Paris. First, pour very carefully into a sherry glass one-half a glassful of Mara-

schino, then introduce the yolk of a raw egg with a spoon without disturbing the Maraschino; next carefully surround the egg with vanilla cordial, and lastly pour a tablespoonful of fine old brandy on top. Be careful not to mix the ingredients. This requires a steady hand, but the drink is heavenly."

MISS VIVIENNE SEGAL, *famous star of light opera.*

"This exquisite mixture has always been my favorite. Three-quarters of a cordial glass full of Benedictine. The balance rich sweet cream. I believe it is known as 'Creme Benedictine'."

JOHN CLARKE, *Ziegfeld star.*

"Side Car Punch, as it is made in London is hard to forget. For a party of ten, slice four oranges and a juicy pineapple into a punch bowl. Pour a bottle of fine Cognac brandy over them and let it steep for a few hours; then pour in three bottles of iced Champagne and serve immediately. A marvelous concoction!"

YVONNE D'ARLE, *musical comedienne.*

"I still prefer the old, reliable Clover Club Cocktail. They are mixing it now even at Deauville. In a shaker place a pony of dry gin, juice of half a lime, white of a raw egg, and a spoonful of Grenadine. Fill with ice, shake and strain into a cocktail glass. When serving it should be garnished with a sprig of fresh mint."

TRIXIE FRIGANZA, *celebrated vaudevillienne.*

"In that nautical city of Venice I first made the acquaintance of a remarkably delicious drink known as 'Port and Starboard'. Pour one-half part Grenadine or raspberry syrup in a cordial glass. Then on top of this pour one-half portion of Creme de Menthe slowly so that the ingredients will not mix. Dear old Venice."

CHARLES ELLIS, Ziegfeld star.

"I have found the Boulevard Cocktail a very pleasing drink. To one part gin, and half a part each of Italian and French Vermouth, add one-half portion orange or grapefruit juice. Ice in a shaker and strain into cocktail glasses. You may try it at the Cafe Rotonde, in Paris."

KARL K. KITCHEN, Broadway's favorite colyumnist.

"My good friend, Harry Craddock, bartender of the Savoy Hotel in London, and dean of all bartenders, braced me up like a new-born infant with a new cocktail he invented for me on the spur of the moment. It is called a 'Hercules,' half gin and half Mati, the Mati coming from Mexico."

CHAPTER XII.

MISCELLANEOUS DRINKS FOR ANYWHERE AND ANYTIME

For Doctor, Lawyer or Indian Chief; Rich Man, Poor Man or Wicked Thief

METROPOLE COCKTAIL

Two parts brandy to one part French Vermouth in a glass. Add two dashes each of ordinary bitters, orange bitters, and gum; fill with cracked ice, mix and pour into cocktail glass.

FORTY-SECOND COUNTRY CLUB

In a shaker put two-thirds Rye whiskey and one-third Italian Vermouth; add a dash of Absinthe. Fill with ice, shake well and serve in cocktail glass.

MANHATTAN COCKTAIL

To one part Rye whiskey add an equal amount of Italian Vermouth (French if dry is preferred), add two dashes bitters, two dashes gum, crushed ice, shake well and serve with a Maraschino cherry.

OLD FASHIONED BRANDY COCKTAIL

In a large whiskey glass place a lump of sugar. Pour

MISCELLANEOUS DRINKS

enough hot water to cover the sugar. Add a lump of ice and two dashes of bitters. Over this pour one portion of brandy. Twist a small piece of lemon peel and place in glass. Stir with small spoon, and serve with spoon in glass.

Rob Roy Cocktail

To two parts Scotch whiskey add one part Vermouth and several dashes of orange bitters. Ice, shake well and strain into cocktail glass.

Rum Cocktail

In a shaker pour two parts rum and one part Vermouth. Add two or three dashes of Angostura bitters, mix well, and serve in cocktail glass.

Whiskey Cocktail

In a shaker, add to each drink of Rye whiskey, two dashes of gum syrup and two dashes of Angostura bitters; fill with ice, shake a few times and strain into a whiskey glass. Add a twist of lemon or lime peel before serving.

Florida Special

Place a cube of ice in a six ounce glass, fill with one pony Bacardi rum, juice of a grapefruit, twist of lime peel, and stir with a highball mixer.

Brandy-Vermouth Cocktail

One part brandy to one part Italian Vermouth, half a spoonful of powdered sugar, a dash of bitters; stir thoroughly until sugar is dissolved. Fill up with cracked ice using Delmonico glass; then fill with seltzer. (If dry cocktail is desired, use French Vermouth and no sugar.)

Vermouth Sec Cocktail

Place in a container one portion of French Vermouth, add two dashes of bitters, fill with ice, mix and strain in a cocktail glass.

Brandy and Ginger Ale

Into a large glass pour a wine-glass of brandy, two or three lumps of ice and fill up with ginger ale; drink while still effervescent.

Cold Irish

Pour into a large glass two wine-glasses of water in which a teaspoonful of fine white sugar has been dissolved, add a wine-glass of Irish whiskey and a large lump of ice; stir with a spoon, and serve very cold.

Split Soda and Brandy

In a medium glass pour a ponyful of brandy and a small lump of ice, squirt full with seltzer water and drink while effervescent.

INDEX

CHAPTER I.
	Page
Brandy Port Nog	11
Brandy Sour	9
Charleston Bracer	9
Dubonnet Cocktail	10
Gin Sour	9
Jamaica Glow	10
Jamaica Bitters	11
Minute Man Highball	11
North and South Cocktail	11
Pearl Cocktail	10
Stinger	10
Tom Collins	10

CHAPTER II.
Alabama Mint Julep	14
Amber Dream	13
Apple Brandy Cocktail	14
Brandy Smash	14
Country Cocktail	14
Havana Special Cocktail	13
Holland Old Fashioned	13
Martini Cocktail	12
Mint Julep	13
Mint Spray Cocktail	12
Orange Blossom Cocktail	12
Orange Blossom Special	12
Tom Gin Martini	13

CHAPTER III.
Albermarle Cocktail	15
Cholera Cocktail	17
Cold Brandy Flip	17
Crimson Cocktail	16
Egg Bacardi Rum Cocktail	17
Egg Nog	15
Egg Whiskey Fizz	16
Gin and Italian	16
Golden Fizz	15
Hot Irish	16
Hot Spiced Rum	15
Sherry and Egg	17
Tom and Jerry	16

CHAPTER IV.
	Page
Brandy and Soda	18
Gin and Italian with Sherry	19
Gin Rickey	19
Jamaica Rum Cocktail	20
Orange Gin Sparkle	18
Palm Beach Special	19
Planter's Punch	19
Plymouth Cocktail	20
Whiskey Fruit Cocktail	19
Whiskey Sour	18
White Plush	18

CHAPTER V.
Alexander Cocktail	21
Coral Cocktail	21
Coronation Cocktail	21
Duchess Cocktail	22
Egg Port Cocktail	22
Fancy Sour Cocktail	23
Orange Curacoa Cocktail	21
Port Wine Flip	22
Pousse Cafe	23
Queen of Ireland	23
Russet Cocktail	22
Sherry Mint Cocktail	22
Vermouth Cocktail	23

CHAPTER VI.
Ambrosia	24
Cider Cocktail	25
Egg Lemonade	26
Iced Sarsaparilla	25
Lemonade	26
Milk and Seltzer	25
Milk Fizz	24
Nectar for Dog Days	24
Oggle Noggle	26
Phosphate Special	26
Purple Nectar	24
Saratoga Cooler	25
Soda Cocktail	25
Soda Nectar	25

CHAPTER VII.
	Page
Absinthe Frappe	27
Bishop	27
Brandy Fizz	27
Brandy Smash	28
Carlton Brandy Cocktail	29
Champagne Cup	30
Cuban Bacardi	30
English Bishop	28
Fancy Whiskey Cocktail	29
Locomotive	29
Peach and Honey	27
Ramos Fizz	28
Sazarac Cocktail	29
Silver Fizz	28
Whiskey Smash	30

CHAPTER VIII.
Baclanova Nectar	33
Champagne Cobbler	33
Champagne Cocktail	33
Claret Cup	32
Mulled Muscatel	31
Port Wine Sangaree	33
Rajah	31
Rhine and Seltzer	32
Sherrio Cocktail	33
Sherry Cobbler	32
Sherry Egg Nog	32

CHAPTER IX.
Brandy Punch	36
Champagne Punch	35
Claret Cup a La Henry VIII	37
Claret Punch	34
El Dorado Punch	37
Hot Brandy and Rum Punch	36
Imperial Punch	37
Milk Punch	36
Nectar Punch	34
Orange Punch	35
Punch a la Romaine	34
Sauterne Punch	35
St. Charles Punch	37

CHAPTER X.
	Page
Blue Blazer	38
Hot Apple Jack	40
Hot Brandy Toddy	40
Hot Gin Sling	39
Hot Irish Whiskey Punch	40
Hot Italian	39
Hot Rum	38
Hot Scotch Punch	40
Hot Whiskey Toddy	39
Port Wine Negus	38
Rock and Rye	39

CHAPTER XI.
Bernie, Ben	41
Clarke, John	42
D'Arle, Yvonne	42
Ellis, Charles	43
Friganza, Trixie	42
Kitchen, Karl K.	43
Lightner, Winnie	41
Segal, Miss Vivienne	42
Tilden, "Big Bill"	41
Winninger, Charles	41

CHAPTER XII.
Brandy and Ginger Ale	46
Brandy-Vermouth Cocktail	46
Cold Irish	46
Florida Special	45
Forty-Second Country Club	44
Manhattan Cocktail	44
Metropole Cocktail	44
Old Fashioned Brandy Cocktail	44
Rob Roy Cocktail	45
Rum Cocktail	45
Split Soda and Brandy	46
Vermouth Sec Cocktail	46
Whiskey Cocktail	45

Notes